MOVING MOUNTAINS

Published in 2024 by OH!
An Imprint of Welbeck Non-Fiction Limited,
part of Welbeck Publishing Group.
Offices in: London – 20 Mortimer Street, London W1T 3JW
and Sydney – Level 17, 207 Kent St, Sydney NSW 2000 Australia
www.welbeckpublishing.com

Disclaimer:

ISBN 978-1-80069-577-1

Compiled and written by: Malcolm Croft
Editorial: Victoria Denne
Project manager: Russell Porter
Production: Arlene Lestrade

A CIP catalogue record for this book is available from the British Library

Printed in Dubai

10 9 8 7 6 5 4 3 2 1

MOVING MOUNTAINS

THE LITTLE GUIDE TO
PINK

UNOFFICIAL AND UNAUTHORIZED

CONTENTS

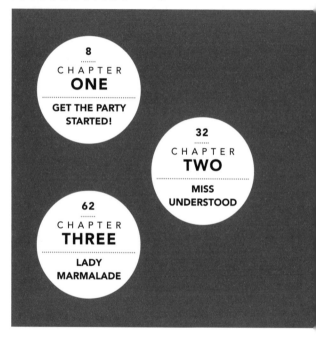

INTRODUCTION

Welcome to the wit, wisdom and wonder-filled world of Alecia Beth Moore's petite but powerful alter-ego – Pink! For more than 25 years (sorry to make you feel old), this rosé-hued "walking conflict" has rubbed against our erogenous zones with a pop-punk personality as raw as it is rude and as candid as it is compassionate. To her millions of fans, Pink represents the perfect popstar: a strong, independent woman who is proudly vulnerable. In one word: relatable.

In Doylestown, Pennsylvania, 1979, Ms Moore was born and was later raised in Philadelphia. Performing on stages from the age of 14, she spent most of her days chillin' out, maxin', relaxin', all cool, taking too many drugs and dropping out from high school. Then, a guy named L.A. Reid (who was up to some good), encouraged her at 16 to move out of her neighbourhood. She signed one little contract, and then changed her career, before moving to California to be a rock star near Bel Air.

From there, Pink, as she from then on became known, released her debut album, *Can't Take Me Home*, at the age of 19. It made her a star. But, of course, that was just the beginning of pop history. The rest has become her story.

Now, with scores of millions of albums sold and sold-out stadiums, Pink's passion for high-energy popsonics and famously acrobatic live performances has yet to yield, wowing crowds old and new with an iconic discography as dynamic and diverse as the singer's almighty vocal range and genre-splitting songs – all while being true to thine self.

This tiny tome is a timely collection of all-star quotes taken from the "smart mouth" and "toothless tiger" herself across interviews from all eras of her enduring career, a daily reminder to be more like Pink and, to quote The Clash's Paul Simonon, remember that "Pink is the true colour of rock and roll." Amen. Enjoy!

CHAPTER
ONE

66

I didn't have a hard childhood. Compared to other people I had a wonderful childhood. But there was a lot of fighting in my house. I was kicked out of Sunday school as a young child, I was kicked out of the Brownies, I never made it to Girl Scouts. I was into punk-rock music and the theme of anti-authority. I believed in all that.

99

Pink, on her upbringing, interview with Ludovic Hunter-Tilney, *Financial Times*, December 8, 2017

It was important to my family that I make my own money. I was a drive-through girl at McDonald's. I had a Janet Jackson microphone – I had power.

Pink, on her formative fast-food career, interview with Ray Isle, *Food & Wine*, October 8, 2018

> "
> I got kicked out of my house when I was 15 years old, I dropped out of school, and six months later I had a record deal. I've been performing ever since.
> "

Pink, on her humble origins, interview with Ray Isle, *Food & Wine*, October 8, 2018

My mom tried to get me to talk to someone when I was 14 to erase all the stuff she put on me. It didn't work. The therapist would ask me about my day, and I'd tell her that at lunch I had a vision of breaking a bottle over someone's head. After the fifth session, she told my mother there was nothing she could do.

Pink, on therapy, interview with Barry Walters, *Rolling Stone*, April 25, 2002

I've been at the homes of friends who are black and been kicked out of their house by their grandmother. I'll walk into a black radio station and, just from the vibe in the room, know that they don't want me there. It's something that's always affected me, and I hate it. I hate the lines that are drawn between people. I hate what society has taught us. I hate history. I didn't do it, but I can do my little part to change things.

Pink, on racial divisions and tensions in America, interview with Barry Walters, *Rolling Stone*, April 25, 2002

I got kicked out of gymnastics when I was 12. I was an ass. I was really competitive. I wouldn't clap if I didn't win first place. The actual remark was 'non-team-like attitude'. I was like, 'Fuck you, I'm out of here, I'm going to be a rock star instead.'

Pink, on her formative dreams of gymnastics glory, interview with Helena de Bertodano, *Daily Telegraph*, December 13, 2012

I was the kid that did all the drugs and no parent wanted their kid to hang out with me. Now parents come up to me and say, 'I love that my kid loves you', and I'm like, 'Wow, that came full circle.'

Pink, on becoming a role model, interview with Annabel Ross, *Rolling Stone*, November 17, 2017

I was 13 when I got into drugs. Eleven if you count weed. I was an early bloomer, but it's good because I stopped young, too. I could be doing all kinds of crazy shit.

Pink, on her drug-taking past, interview with Alison Prato, *Playboy*, December 1, 2002

I want a microphone and an audience. You can keep all the other stuff. I just want to sing. I want a carnival. I'm ready.

Pink, on the only thing she wanted, interview with Roger Coletti, *MTV*, February 8, 2000

I came close to death so many times when I was younger. I've had guns held to my head, all kinds of stuff. I've buried my friends. There are a lot of kids out there who don't have any goals or dreams and it's so easy to get caught up in dangerous crimes. I got out because I always knew what I wanted to do. That's where the balance in my life came from…

Pink, on her adolescent years, interview with Eva Simpson, *Daily Mirror*, February 20, 2003

I'm not going to lie about who I am and what I've done. When I was in seventh grade, it was my philosophy that ecstasy should be handed out in the lunch-line but I totally don't believe that now.

Pink, on ecstasy, interview with Eva Simpson, *Daily Mirror*, February 20, 2003

I would go in still tripping
on acid. I would look at
the burgers and it used
to make me nauseous.

Pink, on working at McDonald's pre-fame, interview with
Sheryl Garrett, *The Face*, December 1, 2002

When I was a little girl, I had this dream in my head that I was going to make incredible music, I was going to change the world, I was going to be rich and famous and gorgeous and skinny and perfect. My life would just be roses and chocolates and various men would fly around the world to see me and I'd have love affairs and wake up in Paris and eat croissants. But I'm still dealing with the fact that anticipation never meets reality.

Pink, on the downsides of fame, interview with Sheryl Garrett, *The Face*, December 1, 2002

I was always climbing trees, skateboarding, all kinds of things. I thought I should have been a boy for a long time, but I'm very glad I'm a girl. I can't imagine walking around with that thing swinging between your legs. How annoying would that be?

Pink, on being a girl, interview with Sheryl Garrett, *The Face*, December 1, 2002

I sang gospel in church at the same time I was in punk rock bands.

Pink, on her earliest singing performances, interview with Jennifer Schonborn, *MTV*, February 19, 2002

I've been clean since '95. Crack and heroin was the two things I didn't do. I saw my friends go there and they never came back.

Pink, on drugs, interview with Paul Rees, *Q Magazine*, February 1, 2004

Me and my mom have always had a candy-coated, selective memory relationship. I love her and she knows that. But she is a lunatic, and she knows that, too.

Pink, on her relationship with her mom, interview with Barry Walters, *Rolling Stone*, April 25, 2002

66

I have always felt famous since I was three. I've always been famous in my head. It's just now other people realize it too.

99

Pink, on fame, interview with Cameron Adams, *Marie Claire*, March 2003

66

When I was growing up, everybody told me I was a fuckup and that I'd end up on a dump heap somewhere.

99

Pink, on music as salvation, interview with Dorian Lynskey, *Blender*, October 15, 2003

She lasted a lot longer than I would have with me as a child. She kicked me out when I was 15. I'd have kicked me out when I was 6!

Pink, on her mother, interview with Dorian Lynskey, *Blender*, October 15, 2003

I like the attention he gives me, and right now I'm his puppy dog. I need to be fed and petted and washed and looked after, and he's very good at telling me how wonderful I am.

Pink, on her early days with then boyfriend Carey Hart, interview with Nick Duerden, *Blender*, December 12, 2002

When I was 13, I kissed a girl I had a big crush on. It was fun. I was on ecstasy. She left me for my brother. I've stayed away from girls ever since.

Pink, on rumours of her sexuality, interview with Alison Prato, *Playboy*, December 1, 2002

CHAPTER
TWO

Why am I a slut and you're the player? You didn't get anything from me that I didn't get from you.

Pink, on the double standards of sex, interview with Logan Hill, *Glamour*, April 29, 2013

I'm pretty confident and, at the same time, I'm pretty insecure. I'm a walking conflict.

Pink, on her contradictory nature, interview with Barry Walters, *Rolling Stone*, April 25, 2002

It was Beatlemania for those boys. I got in trouble for toilet-papering 98 Degrees' bus.

Pink, on the double standards of her first road tour with NSYNC and 98 Degrees, interview with Logan Hill, *Glamour*, April 29, 2013

When I first started, L.A. Reid told me, 'Make sure you put money into your Fuck You account. That's the account that, one day, when people ask you to do things you don't want to do, you say "Fuck you".' I make sure that my Fuck You account is OK, so that I never have to make decisions based on money. I feel like that's where people kill their careers.

Pink, on saving money, interview with Dave Karger, *Entertainment Weekly*, August 24, 2012

People think I'm insane and aggressive and that I'll bite them.

Pink, on her reputation, interview with Joe Coscarelli, *New York Times*, October 5, 2017

I actually ran into Steve Buscemi on the street in New York before my first album came out. I had these big fucking Elton John sunglasses on, pink hair and carried a Pink Panther toy. I went, 'Steve! Mr Pink! I'm Pink! Because of you! I'm going to have an album and you're going to know who I am.' And he was like, 'What the fuck, lady?' and just ran away from me.

Pink, on scaring Steve Buscemi "shitless", interview with Joe Coscarelli, *New York Times*, October 5, 2017

I went through so much clichéd bullshit for the first five years of my career.

Pink, on her earliest days as an R&B star, interview with George Garner, *Music Week*, February 14, 2023

I want to take over this whole fucking world and paint it pink. I'm about to make people forget Madonna.

Pink, on her early career goals, interview with Jon Wiederhorn, *DrDrew.com*, September 19, 2000

After a couple of weeks of crying and throwing up and all that good stuff, I realized that when I always dreamed of being a star it was always by myself, never in a group.

Pink, on leaving the group Choice and going solo, interview with Karen Heller, *Philadelphia Inquirer*, April 5, 2000

I wanted a life different from what I saw my parents go through, struggling to make ends meet, fighting over bills and just bored with their jobs and bored with their lives. I just wanted more. I wanted to see the world, I wanted to conquer it.

Pink, on wanting more from life, interview with Sheryl Garrett, *The Face*, December 1, 2002

We sent a demo tape to LaFace Records through the mail, believe it or not, and they flew us down off the demo tape. I was told when I got there that I'd be singing for L.A. Reid, the boss. I walked into that conference room and there was the entire staff sitting at that table, like 50 people. I almost passed out! So I sang in front of all these people, and L.A. just stood up and threw his pen up in the air and said, 'Where do we sign?'

Pink, on her first audition with LaFace Records boss L.A. Reid, interview with Bill Johnson, *Yahoo! Music*, February 8, 2004

I was the only white girl in our whole clique, and *Reservoir Dogs* was our favourite movie so I became Mr Pink, and my friend was Mr Blonde and there was Mr White, and we were all a bunch of thugs going around the city terrorizing people.

Pink, on the origin of her stage name, interview with Sheryl Garrett, *The Face*, December 1, 2002

I can sing Whitney, I can sing Mary, I can sing Green Day, I can sing Janis Joplin, I can sing Billy Joel, *Phantom Of The Opera*. What genre are you looking for? I can do that!

Pink, on her audition for girl group Choice, interview with Sheryl Garrett, *The Face*, December 1, 2002

It was two long years of
recording and spending
major money, and at the
time I didn't realize it was
all recoupable, so I didn't
give a fuck. But I learned
so much in those years.

Pink, on her time in girl group Choice, interview with
Sheryl Garrett, *The Face*, December 1, 2002

I was this pink haired freak, pissed-off girl with a bad attitude problem, writing songs about bad relationships. But the album wasn't mine. I didn't get to push all the buttons.

Pink, on her debut album *Can't Take Me Home*, interview with Sheryl Garrett, *The Face*, December 1, 2002

I was labelled as trouble so
I was like, 'Trouble? I'll show
you trouble.' They treat
you bad, so you act bad.

Pink, on living up to her label, interview with Karen Coyle,
Faze, July 1, 2002

People see me like the prostitute, the crackhead, the junky, the convict, the runaway, the girl with the attitude.

Pink, on her reputation, interview with Jonathon Moran, *AAP*, April 8, 2004

I was mad at a guy and that's basically the whole first album. I was really mad.

Pink, on the lyrical themes on the album *Can't Take Me Home*, interview with Ray Martin, *A Current Affair*, April 15, 2004

I went from staying up every night and sleeping all day to getting up early, running, getting in shape, getting my lungs right, singing, practicing eight hours a day. In November 1996, I was out all night, all the time. Then a month later, I was in a group, and a month after that, I had a record deal. It happened really fast. It made me believe in fate, almost.

Pink, on her fast-track career path, interview with Bill Johnson, *Yahoo! Music*, February 8, 2004

The thing that drove me to do things was when people told me I couldn't do something. Like, 'You can't sing R&B music 'cause you're white. You can't skate 'cause you're a girl.' I just loved proving people wrong.

Pink, on her defiance, interview with Bill Johnson, *Yahoo! Music*, February 8, 2004

The label wanted me to take etiquette classes, they wanted me to take media coaching, they wanted me to wear dresses. I didn't do it.

Pink, on her record label requesting she act more lady-like, interview with *Herald Sun*, December 2, 2003

The first day I met L.A., he saw me and saw my vision and hugged me and said, 'What's up, superstar?'

Pink, on her first meeting with L.A. Reid, interview with Bill Johnson, *Yahoo! Music*, February 8, 2004

Nobody came to me and said, 'OK, we're going to call you Pink. Here, throw on some pink hair, put on some pink shirts, here you go.' No, this is me. This is who I am.

Pink, her identity, interview with Bill Johnson, *Yahoo! Music*, February 8, 2004

I was signed in 1996, when there was no Britney Spears and Christina Aguilera and Mandy Moore and Jessica Simpson – so everybody didn't know what to think of me. They were like, 'Is she a punk-rocker thug?'

Pink, on being misunderstood as an artist, interview with Bill Johnson, *Yahoo! Music*, February 8, 2004

When I started, it was, 'Is she white, is she black, is she mixed, is she Hispanic?' I'm actually an Irish-German-Lithuanian-Jew.

Pink, on her ethnicity, interview with Paul Rees, *Q Magazine*, February 1, 2004

Everything in this business is designed to encourage you to play along. They know people are so hungry for stardom that they'll just follow the record industry game. I know because I was ready to do anything when I started out.

Pink, on the music industry, interview with Robert Hillburn, *Los Angeles Times*, November 22, 2003

I found that selling records wasn't enough. I told myself after the first record that I'd rather go back home and start over again than be trapped in a one-dimensional world any longer.

Pink, on *Can't Take Me Home*'s musical direction, interview with Robert Hillburn, *Los Angeles Times*, November 22, 2003

CHAPTER
THREE

L.A. and I fought. He was like,
'You can't abandon your fans.'
And I said, 'I want to take them with
me.' He said, 'Fine, I'm going to
give you the opportunity to fail.'

Pink, on L.A. Reid and her musical direction
transformation for *Missundaztood*, interview with Annabel
Ross, *Rolling Stone*, November 17, 2017

It's definitely a switch from the last album. I think people are gonna be shocked! I just had to be all of me instead of just some of me.

Pink, on *Missundaztood*, interview with Jennifer Schonborn, *MTV*, February 19, 2002

I took a lot more control on *Missundaztood*. But I wouldn't have been able to do this record if it weren't for *Can't Take Me Home.* | I wouldn't have known exactly what I wanted if I didn't know what I didn't want. So I had to go through that.

Pink, on her first two albums, interview with Jennifer Schonborn, *MTV*, February 19, 2002

I'd like people who never thought they'd listen to a Pink album to be enlightened about how an artist can take control of her life, do what she wants and fuckin' break the mould and be successful.

Pink, on changing minds, interview with Barry Walters, *Rolling Stone*, April 25, 2002

Rock bottom for me is a catalyst for change.

Pink, on hitting rock bottom, interview with Ludovic Hunter-Tilney, *Financial Times*, December 8, 2017

I found Linda's number in a makeup artist's book, and I left her a 10 minute message about how much I loved her and how she owes me because I got arrested singing her music out of my window at 3:30 in the morning, and how I'm gonna stalk her if she doesn't return my call. She called back five minutes later and said, 'You're fuckin' crazy – you should come over.'

Pink, on song-writing partner Linda Perry, interview with Barry Walters, *Rolling Stone*, April 25, 2002

I just didn't leave. I camped out on her furry rug. We had a goal of writing twenty-five songs. We got to twenty. She became a really, really good friend, and I treasure her. You don't meet a lot of people in L.A. who are so raw and honest.

Pink, on writing *Missundaztood* with Linda Perry, interview with Barry Walters, *Rolling Stone*, April 25, 2002

I didn't write 'Get the Party Started', so you'd have to ask Linda Perry if it's about ecstasy. I don't know what she meant with it. I still don't know if it's 'I'm coming out...' Or 'I'm coming up...' I don't even know what I sang.

Pink, on the meaning of "Get the Party Started", interview with Paul Rees, *Q magazine*, March 2004

I heard it, I loved it.
I loved the vibe. I loved
just everything about it,
from the horns to the way
we sang it. It's a good
song… and I needed it.

Pink, on "Get the Party Started", interview with Jennifer
Schonborn, *MTV*, February 19, 2002

I wanted Linda to help me find the thing I thought music was – lying on the carpet, crying, sharing intimate stories with another person and making music out of it. And I would have rather gone back to working in McDonald's than not do that.

Pink, on her musical direction transformation for *Missundaztood*, interview with Annabel Ross, *Rolling Stone*, November 17, 2017

Missundaztood changed Linda's life, it kind of burst her bubble. She's sort of a tortured artist, she's the real deal. And it wasn't easy on our relationship and it wasn't easy for her.

Pink, on Linda Perry, *Missundaztood* and its massive success, interview with Annabel Ross, *Rolling Stone*, November 17, 2017

I made *Missundaztood* against everyone else's better judgement. I didn't care if it failed because I wasn't happy. I was so disappointed that I had worked my whole life to be this singer and ran away from home – I was homeless for it – and I wasn't representing all of me.

Pink, on *Missundaztood*, interview with Alexandra Pollard, *iNews*, February 17, 2023

When I made *Missundaztood*, I realized I wanted to show people who I really was. I wanted the album to reflect a real person. I was tired of being a marketing concept.

Pink, on *Missundaztood*, interview with Robert Hillburn, *Los Angeles Times*, November 22, 2003

When I went after Linda she was the underdog, and everyone thought I was crazy. And I liked that. And now she's not the underdog anymore.

Pink, on Linda Perry's rise to becoming one of the world's most in-demand songwriters, *Herald Sun*, December 2, 2003

> "
>
> I started writing my own songs because I'd lived 1,000 lives already. I was like, 'You just think I'm some dumb 16-year-old pink-haired punk. No, dude. I've been through a lot of shit and pain.' And I wanted to scream it out.
>
> "

Pink, on wanting to write her own songs, interview with Alexandra Pollard, *iNews*, February 17, 2023

I've always written poetry. I think writing is a requirement for artists. Now, so many artists are so polished, and a lot of them don't write. But I have an awful lot of issues, and I'm just glad they gave me the chance to prove myself. I'm not an artist that gets up and sings love songs.

Pink, on her songwriting, interview with Roger Coletti, *MTV*, February 8, 2000

All my songs come from poetry because I believe that everything, from rap to lyrics, is just poetry in motion. When I was younger, I was very confused and wrote a lot of dark stuff. Now it's more about inspiration. There's more light at the end of the tunnel.

Pink, on writing poetry as song lyrics, interview with Lucy O'Brien, *NME*, January 20, 2000

> **"**
> If I don't get it out, I am going to self-destruct, and I won't be here to make another of your stupid albums. I have to talk about things that mean something to me. **"**

Pink, on changing her musical direction after *Can't Take Me Home*, interview with Katherine Tulich, *Softer*, November 2, 2003

That's why I think *Missundaztood* was so successful because there was no truth in mainstream music. It was surface music… no one was saying anything and that's why people grabbed on to it. I was saying a lot of shit, a lot of stuff that made my parents angry, a lot of stuff that made ex-boyfriends angry and a lot of stuff that made me angry. But it's all true.

Pink, on her second album's mammoth success, interview with Katherine Tulich, *Softer*, November 2, 2003

Five million albums. I can do whatever the hell I want now, and no one will dare stand in my way.

Pink, on the success of *Missundaztood*, interview with Nick Duerden, *Blender*, December 12, 2002

I called it that to piss my teachers off because they annoyed me.

Pink, on the misspelling of *Missundaztood*, interview with Simon Amstell, *Popworld*, January 21, 2001

> **"** I think we all feel misunderstood, and our main goal is to be appreciated for all that we are – most of the time we don't even understand ourselves. **"**

Pink, on why she called her second album *Missundaztood*, interview with Karen Coyle, *Faze*, July 1, 2002

We're kindred spirits. It was natural, it was weird, it was scary, it was exciting, it was love. I mean, we'd argue, but it was just like a relationship, and this album was our kid.

Pink, on her songwriting with Linda Perry for *Missundaztood*, interview with Neil Strauss, *Blender*, July 2002

I'm very, very proud of *Missundaztood*, it's a lot of fun. Anyone out there expecting *Can't Take Me Home* will be shocked and I hope pleasantly surprised. I went a little old school and made real music without having to pay producers before they'd work with me. I went after people that completely inspired me and whom I looked up to and it was a magical experience. Some of it's sad, but I don't mean to make any of you suicidal.

Pink, on *Missundaztood*, *Capital Radio FM Takeover*, January 3, 2002

"

I would say about
25 per cent of what they
say about me is true.

"

Pink, on the media, interview with Jonathon Moran,
AAP, April 8, 2004

I can't put my music into a category. My favourite word is 'eclectic' because I have so many different influences. So the music is really versatile.

Pink, on defining her music, interview with Bill Johnson, *Yahoo! Music*, February 8, 2004

I didn't think *Missundaztood* was going to be that commercially successful. But it taught me to trust my instincts more. I don't really judge my success on how many records I sell, though. I judge it on how much fun I have and if I can look in a mirror and say, 'Okay, you took a risk and you believed in it and you stood up for it.'

Pink, on *Missundaztood's* success, *Music Connection*, January 9, 2004

❝

Missundaztood was an album of complete nakedness, Linda stripped me of all my clothing.

❞

Pink, on writing songs with Linda Perry for *Missundaztood*, interview with Kate Spicer, *The Observer*, November 9, 2003

Missundaztood gave me a sense of freedom and purpose. It allowed me to exorcize a lot of my demons. The world has become my therapist. And it helped me to feel better about being an outcast, knowing that there's so many other people that share my pain.

Pink, on *Missundaztood*, interview with Wes Orshoski, *New York Times*, November 8, 2003

I've fought for my credibility in this pop world. I was never the popular kid, God dammit, but I am now.

Pink, on popularity, interview with Wes Orshoski, *New York Times*, November 8, 2003

CHAPTER
FOUR

I accept the challenge that kids are gonna be relating to me more so than a lot of other artists because I am telling the truth. I've been there.

Pink, on her relatability, *ABC News*, November 6, 2003

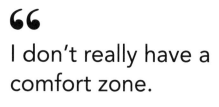

I don't really have a comfort zone.

Pink, on feeling OK with feeling uncomfortable, interview with Sam Damshenas, *Gay Times*, February 24, 2023

Writing, singing and performing, it's my therapy and my shows are group therapy where we all get to come and feel our feelings.

Pink, on her live shows, interview with Sam Damshenas, *Gay Times*, February 24, 2023

You see me as a strong woman; therefore, I must be a lesbian or I must be a guy? Really, that's the best you've got? It's all so fucking ridiculous. Why is that an insult to me?

Pink, on people who question her "butch" sexuality, interview with Sam Damshenas, *Gay Times*, February 24, 2023

Hatred and division is such a waste. Why are we fighting love? I think life is more fun when you have the freedom to live it how you choose… Homophobic people are missing out on a lot of fun.

Pink, on homophobia, interview with Sam Damshenas, *Gay Times*, February 24, 2023

I know what I want. And I'm not giving out any favours. I gotta get mine. That's the kind of girl I am.

Pink, on who she is, interview with Barry Walters, *Rolling Stone*, April 25, 2002

I'm never the kind of person who's sitting at home reading the charts and basing how I feel about myself or even my career on stats. I've always based it on, 'Am I doing the best that I can do?'

Pink, on her career, interview with Dave Karger, *Entertainment Weekly*, August 24, 2012

I have very thick skin. I do what I want. I can handle criticism; it doesn't move my needle. It hurts my feelings, I guess – or it used to. But it doesn't change my actions.

Pink, on having thick skin, interview with Molly Creeden, *Women's Health*, February 8, 2023

> **"**
> I've never won the popularity contest. I was never as big as Britney or Christina. If you look at any paragraph about pop music, I don't get mentioned – my name doesn't come up. And yet, here I go again…
> **"**

Pink, on her enduring legacy and career, interview with Joe Coscarelli, *New York Times*, October 5, 2017

There's a lot of anger in my songs. Everything inspires my anger.

Pink, on her anger, interview with Dominic Mohan, *The Sun*, November 30, 2002

When I was 21, I was a dysfunctional, broken puppy. I was so righteously angry and just had no focus on where to put my anger. It was just a fireball. 'I'm gonna fucking blaze a path through this world, and I'm gonna inspire people to come with me.' And, you know, now I'm 43, sometimes I'm like, 'Dude, what did you do?'

Pink, on her formative years as a popstar, interview with Alexandra Pollard, *iNews*, February 17, 2023

I was watching a VH1 ranking of the 25 sexiest rock stars. I was number seven. The guy goes, 'Pink looks tough, like she'll slap you around all night.' Carey and I were in bed, about to go to sleep. I was like, 'We can't go to sleep. I have to slap you around all night.' We just laughed, rolled over and went to sleep.

Pink, on her tough reputation, interview with Alison Prato, *Playboy*, December 1, 2002

You don't see me apologize
a lot because 99.9 per cent
of the time I mean what
I said, so you're just gonna
have to hate me harder.

Pink, on remaining true to herself, interview with
Alexandra Pollard, *iNews*, February 17, 2023

I think there are a lot of sides to me. I'm very outgoing. I don't hold my tongue. I could be feeling two completely different ways at the same time. I'm hard to explain. I'm a book by myself.

Pink, trying to define herself, interview with Jon Wiederhorn, *DrDrew.com*, September 19, 2000

I wake up ready for war, ready for someone to do something fucked-up.

Pink, on her war mindset, interview with Nick Duerden, *Blender*, December 12, 2002

I am butch, aren't I? I'm becoming a gay icon, and I love it. It's probably my short hair and attitude.

Pink, on her gay icon status, interview with Nick Duerden, *Blender*, December 12, 2002

I think I've helped a lot of girls let go of the need to dress in a slutty way.

Pink, on the lasting impact of her songs, interview with Dominic Mohan, *The Sun*, November 30, 2002

I'm a toothless tiger. I got
a big bark and no bite.

Pink, on her reputation, interview with Sheryl Garrett,
The Face, December 1, 2002

I honestly can't remember thinking I'd do anything else on this earth than make music. I'm so anti-authority that I could never have a regular job. I've always been into poetry and arts and dancing and drinking and it seemed like the only thing, it just seemed natural.

Pink, on her career as destiny, interview with Sheryl Garrett, *The Face*, December 1, 2002

"

I don't know why people like me, I never really figured that out.

"

Pink, on her fanbase, interview with Ray Martin, *A Current Affair*, April 15, 2004

As long as we have the
presidents that we have
and the world the way
it's going, there's always
something to rebel against
and keep me busy!

Pink, on the state of the world, interview with Ray Martin,
A Current Affair, April 15, 2004

People know that I'm not Barbie, and I'm all right with that. There's a lot of pressure on women and kids to look and be a certain way, and I don't agree with that. It's nauseating, it's depressing and it makes people suicidal. So I was trying to change that. You don't have to be skinny and beautiful – you've just gotta have charm and personality, baby. And a good pair of fuck-me heels.

Pink, on being a role model for her fans, interview with Dorian Lynskey, *Blender*, October 15, 2003

I'll be in a rage sometimes because I can't get it all out, so I have to write. Writing is my medicine. If I didn't write, I don't know what I'd do. I'd like to have a punching bag… but songwriting is my punching bag.

Pink, on songwriting, interview with Bill Johnson, *Yahoo! Music*, February 8, 2004

People totally think
I'm mixed race, like
I'm a mutt. But we
all are. We're all pink
on the inside.

Pink, on her race, interview with Bill Johnson,
Yahoo! Music, February 8, 2004

I enjoyed fame for a while because I like attention. But I soon realized what attention matters and what doesn't. Attention from my family and dogs is important. The attention from the world putting me on a pedestal for everyone to throw rocks at, I can do without.

Pink, on fame, interview with Simon Amstell, *Popworld*, January 31, 2004

For the most part, just
being me has kept
the idiots away.

Pink, on intimidation as a tactic, interview with *Bliss
magazine*, December 1, 2003

If I was ever completely happy, I'd be completely useless.

Pink, on happiness, interview with Jim Farber, *Entertainment Weekly*, November 15, 2003

When anything works people try to copy it. I just think it's way more fun to have the opportunity to fail. I'd be so bored following in someone else's footsteps. I like being an innovator.

Pink, on being an innovator, interview with Cameron Adams, *Marie Claire*, March 2003

The good thing where I'm at right now is that I'm 24 years old, and I've done everything I said I was going to do when I was a little girl. Now, it's just about having fun and causing chaos, and doing whatever I want to do.

Pink, on defeating her career goals, interview with *Herald Sun*, December 2, 2003

I've always been very confident but success has created some insecurities. In high school, there was only 400 people judging you. You can easily go 'Fuck off!' to 400 people. But when it's 400 million judging you and I read articles saying, 'Her once-taut tummy now hangs above her belt!', I'm like 'Fuck dude, I'm still a girl. Give me a break!'.

Pink, on her insecurity, interview with Simon Amstell, *Popworld*, January 31, 2004

When I get to the top, I'm sure I'll be a multi-millionaire, but that's not what I really care about. As long as I can pay my way, buy Perrier instead of Evian, I'm cool.

Pink, on shunning materialism, interview with Dominic Mohan, *The Sun*, November 30, 2002

My idea of a perfect day would be waking up in my bed, whenever I want. And then I would walk to the beach and run into the ocean. I don't know if clothes would be involved or not. And then there would be a really sexy surfer guy waiting for me in the water.

Pink, on her perfect day, interview with Capital Radio FM *Takeover*, January 3, 2002

I'm proof that things absolutely can happen. Nobody thought that I would get to here. I was determined to make it, to do something with my life, from the age of seven. I just wanted out.

Pink, on manifesting her destiny, interview with Dominic Mohan, *The Sun*, November 30, 2002

I can kick ass, but I come in peace.

Pink, on being tough, interview with Jon Wiederhorn, *DrDrew.com*, September 19, 2000

66

There is no demographic for me. It's young, old, moms, daughters, every colour of the rainbow, from every part of life. Everyone can relate to me. It's cool.

99

Pink, on her diverse audience, interview with Lucy O'Brien, *NME*, January 20, 2000

CHAPTER
FIVE

Last time I was completely changing direction, going out on a limb and taking a chance, everyone was really hesitant. This time around they were like, 'Do what you want'. And that bothered me because I love doing exactly what I can't do!

Pink, on contradicting people's expectations for *Try This*, interview with Cameron Adams, *Marie Claire*, March 2003

It always just feels like there's a missing piece somewhere, and I have to find that person. And then when I do it, it flows like water.

Pink, on finding the perfect collaborator for her albums, interview with *Music Connection*, January 9, 2004

Imagine this hardcore punk rocker coming up and saying, 'I've got some songs for you'. I'm like 'All right, what the hell is that going to sound like?' I was intrigued.

Pink, on working with Rancid's Tim Armstrong for *Try This*, interview with Cameron Adams, *Marie Claire*, March 2003

When I was making *Try This*, I had a lot of attitude. I didn't want to make another album so soon after the last one, which arrived precisely two years ago. I thought, 'I want to live another 20 years, so I have something to write about.'

Pink, on writing and recording *Try This* with Tim Armstrong, interview with Jim Farber, *Entertainment Weekly*, November 15, 2003

I needed new blood. And Tim's an underdog, just like Linda was an underdog. Now she's too busy for me.

Pink, on her *Try This* partner Tim Armstrong, and Linda Perry, interview with Jim Farber, *Entertainment Weekly*, November 15, 2003

I named the album *Try This*, because the way I was raised was to try new things, even if everyone else thinks you're crazy.

Pink, on the title of her third album, *AOL*, December 1, 2003

Britney and Christina Aguilera's image has changed so much over the last few years.
I think they are copying me.
Some people have their own identity and others don't.

Pink, on other stars copying her image, interview with Dominic Mohan, *The Sun*, November 30, 2002

I figured when I dropped out of high school, I'd never have to deal with politics, I'd never have to deal with business, I'd never had to answer to anyone. And now here I am, doing all of those things. The music business is politics, it's all about business.

Pink, on the music business, interview with Sheryl Garrett, *The Face*, December 1, 2002

It's fun pissing people off. And it's gotten really interesting since becoming famous, because now people are scared of me.

Pink, on pissing people off, interview with Nick Duerden, *Blender*, December 12, 2002

I want to prove to myself that I can do this and still raise a daughter that likes me when she's 12, and that I can have a marriage that lasts, unlike anyone in my family, and I can be played on Top 40 radio as a woman over 35, and I can become a better person than I was last night on Twitter. I am a crazy person that seeks to be better.

Pink, on being the best she can be, interview with Annabel Ross, *Rolling Stone*, November 17, 2017

For anyone that's been with me for a while, I feel like we're all growing up together. Those people know me in and out. They know my intentions, what I stand for, my sense of humour, all that. The rest of the world? Not at all.

Pink, on her closest friends and family, interview with George Garner, *Music Week* interview, February 14, 2023

People ask me, 'Do you think it's better for women now?' And I have no idea. I would love to talk to younger girls that are coming up in this business. The way it is in 2023? I have no idea.

Pink, on females in the modern music industry, interview with Alexandra Pollard, *iNews*, February 17, 2023

People always try to threaten me with their opinions. Well, fuck you, I don't make music for you.

Pink, on people who force their opinions of her on her, interview with Sam Damshenas, *Gay Times*, February 24, 2023

I'm a selfish songwriter, I write about my problems.

Pink, on songwriting, interview with Ludovic Hunter-Tilney, *Financial Times*, December 8, 2017

Fame ends up being its own beautifully adorned cage. Being a singer has been awesome and awful – everything I thought it could be and more.

Pink, on fame, interview with Ray Isle, *Food and Wine*, October 8, 2018

When it's just me and a guitar and I do 'Fuckin' Perfect' and I see grown men crying and mums hugging their daughters, it's real, it's real shit.

Pink, on the power of her performing live, interview with Annabel Ross, *Rolling Stone*, November 17, 2017

I don't live in the Hollywood bubble. I never have and I never will. I wasn't invited to that party. And if I was, I'd probably arrive late and be dressed inappropriately.

Pink, on breaking free from the popstar cliché, interview with Helena de Bertodano, *Daily Telegraph*, December 13, 2012

I don't see limits. I don't see the end of the road as the end of the road. I just see it as a place to start building. I bite off more than I can chew. I ferociously attack life.

Pink, on her attitude to living life out loud, interview with Molly Creeden, *Women's Health*, February 8, 2023

One show, I saw this bearded biker in leather standing next to a drag queen, and you could tell they didn't wanna be next to each other. By the end of the show, they were arm-in-arm, sweating together, crying together and laughing together, having an experience that probably changed both of them – and me, in the process. It's fucking beautiful. It's magic.

Pink, on the inclusivity of her live shows, interview with Sam Damshenas, *Gay Times*, February 24, 2023

My fans and I have been growing up together since the first album. I'm 43 now, and each album has been a chapter in our lives and we're walking through it together.

Pink, on growing up with her fans, interview with Sam Damshenas, *Gay Times*, February 24, 2023

"

I like being strong. I identify with my core, my intuition and my strength. I have wide, big feet, and I joke, 'The better to kick you with.' I'm short, close to the ground, fast and agile.

"

Pink, on her size and strength, interview with Molly Creeden, *Women's Health*, February 8, 2023

There's been many mornings when I look at myself in the mirror with tears in my eyes and I'm like, 'You can't have it all'. There's always a compromise.

Pink, on compromise, interview with Joe Coscarelli, *New York Times*, October 5, 2017

CHAPTER
SIX

Since I grew up in a broken home, the one thing I wanted was a family that somehow would work.

Pink, on wanting to start a family, interview with Ray Isle, *Food & Wine*, October 8, 2018

"

Statistically you
can't be a pop star
if you're over 35.

"

Pink, on growing old in the music industry, interview with
Ludovic Hunter-Tilney, *Financial Times*, December 8, 2017

66

If the world is ending then screw it, let's dance.

99

Pink, on the end of the world, interview with Sam Damshenas, *Gay Times*, February 24, 2023

My daughter asked me the other day, 'Why do you do this?' and I said, 'It's in me and I feel like I have a responsibility.'

Pink, on music as her purpose, interview with Sam Damshenas, *Gay Times*, February 24, 2023

Somebody asked Carey how I've changed since I had Willow, and he said my claws have sharpened. They got longer, too.

Pink, on motherhood, interview with Logan Hill, *Glamour*, April 29, 2013

Being a parent is a Jedi mind fuck. It's also the raddest thing ever.

Pink, on becoming a parent, interview with Logan Hill, *Glamour*, April 29, 2013

> **"**
> I make noise for a living
> so it's important for my
> mental health to unplug
> and be in nature.
> **"**

Pink, on her love of being in the great outdoors, interview with Molly Creeden, *Women's Health*, February 8, 2023

Every performance I get to do new things, so I'm always trying to top it. But it's going to start getting really hard to do that because I've done the craziest stuff. But we're always on the lookout for new cool things that you might not die from.

Pink, on her aerial acrobatics during her live shows, interview with Molly Creeden, *Women's Health*, February 8, 2023

> **"**
>
> I start at the end of the stage, and I'm thinking, 'When did Willow last have her cold medicine?' And I think, I might be sad. Then I get thrown into the air and I'm like, 'AHHH!!! I'M NOT SAD ANYMORE!!!' It's awesome.
>
> **"**

Pink, on her aerial acrobatics during her live shows, interview with Molly Creeden, *Women's Health*, February 8, 2023

Carey fell 40 ft and broke
14 bones the day I met him.
I thought he was dead.

Pink, on her husband Carey Hart, interview with Helena
de Bertodano, *Daily Telegraph*, December 13, 2012

After drinking a couple Red Bulls, I held up a board saying, 'Will you marry me?'

Pink, on proposing to her boyfriend Carey Hart on April 1 while he was racing in a competition, interview with Fleur East, *Planet Radio*, February 24, 2023

This is the dream I had when I was four, and now I've done it. I no longer feel like the underdog with a point to prove. My husband is like, 'Hey, it only took you nine years to get people to like you.' I'm like, 'It took me nine years to like you, too…'

Pink, on her career and her husband Carey Hart, interview with Helena de Bertodano, *Daily Telegraph*, December 13, 2012

I went to a Cher concert and I saw all the dancers, who were doing these incredible silks and I was like, 'Well, why isn't a singer doing that? Why hasn't a singer done this? Why do they get to have all the fun?'

Pink, on pioneering aerial acrobatics in her live shows, CBS *Sunday Morning*, October 8, 2017

I feel like grief is like a suitcase that you never stop unpacking. And I haven't even opened up that suitcase yet. I've lost a lot of people in my life. But this time, I lost my dad and a dear friend within eight months of each other, and I just wonder where they went. I want to think they're somewhere. It's a sweet idea.

Pink, on grief, and the death of her beloved father/ manager Jim Moore, interview with Alexandra Pollard, *iNews*, February 17, 2023

Smoking is the only vice I have left. A pack a day since I was 9. I know I should stop smoking as well, but it scares me. I mean, what would I turn to next?

Pink, on vices, and her then smoking habit, interview with Nick Duerden, *Blender*, December 12, 2002

I'm the official winemaker for Two
Wolves, our estate. It's a gorgeous
property. It was 18 acres of vineyard,
already certified organic, when we
moved in; now we're at 25 acres. The
first year we harvested three tons of
grapes; now we're up to 18. I prune
vines while listening to Beck. I could
make wine for the rest of my life.

Pink, on her Two Wolves Estate wine, interview with
Ray Isle, *Food & Wine*, October 8, 2018

> **"**
>
> I remember looking at my dad in the front seat and him going, 'Honey, you just put your head back, spit in the wind, and show them what you got.' And he raised me that way. He was a Vietnam vet. He was tough, and he raised me like that, but he was also a poet, a folk singer and he knew the language of the trees. He gave me all of that. He was always so proud of me.
>
> **"**

Pink, on her father, and her now-legendary 2009 Grammy performance, interview with George Garner, *Music Week Interview*, February 14, 2023

I don't have sexual feelings toward women. I like Carey's penis too much, so that pretty much rules out the whole lesbian thing, doesn't it?

Pink, on rumours of her sexuality, interview with Nick Duerden, *Blender*, December 12, 2002

My advice is to take three deep breaths, do what the hell you want and try to make it to 21. Then you can decide what you want to do with the rest of your life.

Pink, on her life advice, interview with Dominic Mohan, *The Sun*, November 30, 2002

I was terrified of having a daughter, because of the relationship with my own mum, but I think children are the greatest teachers. Willow makes me stop and think... and she's allergic to injustice.

Pink, on her daughter Willow, interview with Fleur East, *Planet Radio*, February 24, 2023

Right now all the scripts that people are sending me are like the juvie, the convict, the runaway, the tough girl with an attitude. I would like to really act if I'm in a movie and not just play myself. I need a challenge. I want to play the girl next door that's cute and sweet and doesn't curse. I'd be really good at playing, like, an 80-year-old senile woman.

Pink, on her movie acting aspirations, interview with
Music Connection, January 9, 2004

I just don't believe in grudges anymore. I'm too tired. I have two kids.

Pink, on her infamous conflicts with other artists and label bosses, interview with Rebecca Nicholson, *Guardian*, October 13, 2017

"

Sometimes I want to make a really shitty record and get dropped and go start a band and write a death-metal opera.

"

Pink, on death metal operas, interview with Wes Orshoski, *New York Times*, November 8, 2003

I'm Rocky Balboa; I'm from Philadelphia, I have a fighter mentality.

Pink, on her fighter mindset, interview with Rebecca Nicholson, *The Guardian*, October 13, 2017

The Grammys 2009 was my a-ha moment. It was one of those nights where you're looking back and you're talking to your grandkids and you're like, 'Yeah, I had that night where everyone stood up and I felt awesome. It was that moment where I felt like finally, I had been given my due a little bit.'

Pink, on her Grammy 2009 performance of "Glitter in the Air", interview with *Canton Repository*, November 23, 2010

I named the album *Beautiful Trauma* because life is fucking traumatic. There's natural disasters at every turn and there's kids starving and there's Trump and there's all kinds of stuff going on, but there's beautiful people in the world that are having a blast and being good to each other and helping others. Because I can be dark, I try to constantly remind myself that there's more good than bad.

Pink, on the album *Beautiful Trauma*, interview with Rebecca Nicholson, *Guardian*, October 13, 2017

As soon as the baby can say 'mama', I'm going on the road. We are going to be a travelling family gypsy band with garlands in our hair.

Pink, on her love of performing live, *Canton Repository*, November 23, 2010

We make a Grenache rosé, which is fantastic. But I refuse to release it. If I put a pink wine out first? 'Pink's rosé?' That'd be awful!

Pink, on her "second dream", a vineyard in California called Two Wolves Wines, interview with Ray Isle, *Food & Wine*, October 8, 2018

> **"**
>
> When I was a little girl, all I wanted to do was make one hit record. To be able to put out an album full of them is pretty damn special.
>
>

Pink, on her Greatest Hits album, interview with *Canton Repository*, November 23, 2010

It's really hard for one song to represent a whole Pink album, because a whole Pink album doesn't make sense. The only common thread is my voice. You're going to have rock and roll, you're going to have R&B. You're going to have a country ballad and a folk song and a pop, Max Martin, radio-friendly hit. So I think that's kind of the mystery bag, that's what's fun.

Pink, on her albums' variedness, interview with James Montgomery, *MTV*, July 17, 2012